Caroline Bowen

Developmental Phonological Disorders

A practical guide for families and teachers

ACER PRESS

To Isobel and Frederick Hart

First published 1998
by The Australian Council for Educational Research Ltd
19 Prospect Hill Road, Camberwell, Melbourne, Victoria 3124
Reprinted 1998

Copyright © 1998 Caroline Bowen

All rights reserved. Except under the conditions described in the Copyright Act 1968 of Australia and subsequent amendments, no part of this publication may be reproduced, stored in a retrieval system or transmitted in any form or by any means, electronic, mechanical, photocopying, recording or otherwise, without the written permission of the publishers.

Edited by Katherine Steward
Cover designed by Rob Cowpe
Printed by Gill Miller Press Pty Ltd

National Library of Australia
Cataloguing-in-Publication data:

Bowen, Caroline Margaret.
Developmental phonological disorders: a practical guide for families and teachers.

Bibliography
ISBN 0 86431 1256 3.

1. Articulation disorders in children. 2. Articulation disorders in children – Treatment. 3. Speech disorders in children. 4. Speech therapy for children. I. Title.

618.9285506

Editorial preface

There is a long-standing tradition in the field of speech-language pathology to view phonological remediation as something that takes place between a child and their speech-language pathologist. In recent years, there have been efforts made to expand this process to include parents and teachers. This expanded context is well-reasoned. For one thing, a child's motivation to change will be tied to their ability to communicate with both their family and peers. Additionally, the time needed for phonological remediation is greater than that available on the case loads of speech-language pathologists.

Dr Bowen has made a significant contribution to the practice of phonological remediation. She has developed a clearly stated and manageable program that gives the parent a valuable role in the process. An important part of such a program, however, needs to be an effective means to explain the program to parents. Her *Developmental Phonological Disorders: A Practical Guide for Families and Teachers* does just this.

Dr Bowen's guide begins by outlining very clearly the major milestones of phonetic and phonological acquisition. The discussion of phonetic development introduces the parent to the use of phonetic symbols and the fact that speech sounds are acquired in a particular sequence. Subsequently, the guide describes how these speech sounds form a system that includes the child's ability to perceive words and their ability to produce them. The errors that children make can then be understood as a set of phonological processes that children use to simplify the underlying representations of their words. It is pointed out that these processes have a developmental sequence as well. These points are made at an appropriate level of detail which includes well organised and readable tables.

The second half of the guide is devoted to explaining the treatment program. A central part of this section is the inclusion of a series of questions that parents ask, taken from Dr Bowen's extensive experience as a speech-language pathologist. I can't help but believe that parents will find this format an effective way to answer their own questions about how they can contribute to their child's remediation. The parental questions are then followed by an outline of the program itself, including descriptions of metalinguistic training, auditory bombardment, and special techniques such as modelling and labelled praise. It concludes with the advice that as learning is gradual, so the child's progress will be gradual.

There is one further point I would like to make about this guide. Both it and the author's remediation program have been shown to be effective. This was done through carefully controlled research as described in detail in her recent doctoral dissertation at Macquarie University. It is an outstanding work and validates the treatment approach outlined here. In closing, it is a pleasure to recommend Dr Bowen's guide, and I am confident that it will be widely used.

DAVID INGRAM
UNIVERSITY OF BRITISH
COLUMBIA

Foreword

Caroline Bowen has pioneered research into establishing the efficacy of phonological therapy for children with developmental phonological disorders. This book seeks to put this work to practical use by providing a guide for families and teachers. It is also packed with information, advice and guidance for clinicians. It establishes as a first principle the importance of communicating accurate information about the nature of the disorder to families, and emphasises the value of involving families and teachers in the therapeutic process.

Dr Bowen puts forward the view that speech-language pathologists should confidently use quite technical terms when talking to parents about their child's problems. This approach, she suggests, enables parents to better understand the nature of the disorder and the reasons for the type of therapeutic regime being employed. This involves giving parents information about the normal speech sound system of English and about the process of normal speech development, especially the characteristic patterns in children's speech production throughout the period of speech development. Fundamental to this approach is the view that this disorder is developmental and phonological. The author is unequivocal in her presentation of the relevant information on this point. The manner in which she expounds this view is a model of clear communication that will assist clinicians in their interactions with families and teachers.

On the basis of this information, parents have a framework within which they can understand the need for general and detailed assessment as a basis for planning therapy. Clinicians can thus feel confident of parental support for the in-depth analysis that is required in undertaking a clinical phonological assessment, which will identify the patterns in a child's speech production and their developmental status. It is on the basis of such an assessment that therapy can be planned. As Dr Bowen emphasises, phonological therapy must be individualised, therefore detailed assessment is essential.

Embarking on a treatment program with a child who has a severe developmental phonological disorder is a serious and somewhat daunting task for all concerned: the child and his or her family; the child's teacher(s); and of course the therapist. Dr Bowen counsels openness in this endeavour. She explains the nature of phonological processes in children's speech development detailing both their phonetic description and their developmental status. While this approach involves using technical terms and fairly complex concepts, this information is imparted to the adults involved in a clear and accessible manner. This information is essential for the success of the therapeutic approach, as involving parents and teachers is a key element in ensuring phonological changes and progress.

When parents and teachers have this detailed background they are able to contribute to the treatment program in an informed way. Their participation, however, also depends on an understanding of the therapeutic approach and the treatment procedures. These are both explained by the author in highly accessible language. In an informative question-and-answer section (pages 15-19) the nature of developmental phonological disorder and the effects of treatment are outlined. Following this are detailed descriptions of the most common techniques in phonological therapy: auditory bombardment and minimal contrast therapy. With an understanding of these techniques parents and teachers can more readily carry out homework exercises and facilitate generalisation and carry-over into everyday speech.

With an apt sense of realism Dr Bowen provides examples of therapeutic interactions that can easily, if not effortlessly, be incorporated into everyday conversations between children and adults. Modelling and feedback are presented as natural elements in parental and teaching behaviours that can be appropriately modified to promote phonological change and reinforce phonological progress. In this regard, in particular, the author indicates the importance of empowering parents though knowledge and skills to be proactive in the treatment of their child and in the monitoring of his or her development. This situation can only be brought about, however, if the therapist is prepared to share information with parents and to spend time training them in the use of specific treatment techniques. Given the traditional therapy program of once-weekly therapy sessions this is an eminently sensible approach.

In conclusion the author makes some key points for parents, emphasising that language learning is a gradual process. This book is an extremely valuable resource for clinicians, families and teachers. As such it will provide effective assistance for children whose communication development is impaired by what Dr Bowen rightly asserts is a 'very "treatable" language disorder'.

PAMELA GRUNWELL
DE MONTFORT UNIVERSITY

Contents

Editorial preface *David Ingram*	iii
Foreword *Pamela Grunwell*	v
List of tables	viii
1 Introduction for parents and teachers	1
2 Phonetic development	4
The sequence of phonetic development	4
Voiced or voiceless?	4
Patterns of speech sounds	5
3 Phonological development	7
Speech perception	7
Speech production	7
Organisation of the speech sound system	10
When is a phonological process considered to be normal?	11
4 Speech-language pathology treatment	13
Readiness	13
Communication assessment	14
Questions families often ask about phonological therapy	15
5 Phonological therapy	20
Parent education and training	20
Metalinguistic training	20
Phonetic production training	21
Multiple exemplar training	21
Auditory bombardment	21
Minimal contrast therapy	23
Homework	23
Homework sessions	24
6 The role of preschool and school teachers	25
Preschool	25
7 Special techniques for helping	27
Modelling	27
Modelling corrections	27
Revisions and repairs	28
Judgment of correctness	31
Reinforcement	32
Labelled praise	33
Tokens	33
Rewarding homework	33
Story time	34
8 Some important points	35
Research background	37
References	38
Selected Bibliography	39

Tables

1	Expressive language development	3
2	How well words can be understood by parents	3
3	Normal phonetic development	5
4	Contrasting speech sounds at the beginning of words	6
5	Contrasting speech sounds within and at the end of words	6
6	Examples of phonological processes in normal speech development	8
7	Chronology of phonological processes in normal speech sound development	12
8	Auditory bombardment lists	22
9	Auditory bombardment lists using word pairs and three-word contrasts	22

Introduction for parents and teachers

Developmental phonological disorders (or phonological disability) are a group of language disorders that affect children's ability to develop speech that is easily understood by the time they are 4 years old, because the sound patterns of language are disrupted. Even though the cause or causes of developmental phonological disorders remain unknown, it has been successfully treated by speech-language pathologists since the 1930s. Children with speech that is unintelligible or difficult to understand, due to developmental phonological disorders, are generally developing quite normally in every other respect, and do not have serious physical problems. They usually understand what is said to them, have adequate vocabularies, and can string sentences together at least as well as other children of the same age.

Grammatical development and use may be slower than normal in children with phonological disability. Sometimes it is hard for adults to determine whether a child is just having difficulty with sound patterns, or with sound patterns and grammatical rules. For example, it can be impossible to tell whether some phonologically disabled children are applying grammatical rules such as 's' plurals (e.g. two dogs, two cats), 's' possessive markers (e.g. dog's bone, cat's whiskers) and regular past tense verbs (e.g. dog jumped, cat purred), because of the way their words are pronounced. Certain children with developmental phonological disorders never use the sounds /s/ and /d/ at the ends of words, so it may not be possible to ascertain whether they know about grammatical word endings or not.

Research into the nature, causes and management of developmental phonological disorders has, until recently, taken a back seat while more pervasive, handicapping communication disorders have been studied. During the past 10 to 15 years, however, speech-language pathology practice in the area of children's speech sound disorders has been increasingly influenced by the interest that linguists have been taking in clinical phonology. Clinical phonology is the application of linguistic principles and theory to language disorders affecting speech sound systems.

From the research done so far, it is clear that more needs to be known about normal speech and language development, and the mechanism that underlies the failure of some 4 year olds to develop clear intelligible speech.

In normal development, children who are learning to talk have to conquer the complexities of language comprehension, vocabulary, grammar, syntax and so on, as well as having to learn how to speak intelligibly. Additionally, children have to devote time and energy to other important areas of development, such as acquiring motor and social skills. All of this learning usually takes place gradually, with the emphasis constantly shifting from one developmental area to another. If an area of development, such as learning to organise and produce the sound patterns of language, poses particular difficulty for a child (as in the case of a child with phonological disability), then the development of clear speech will be even more gradual than usual. Indeed, speech progress may come to a complete standstill.

Children with developmental phonological disorders need skilled help to master the sound system of their native language. This help, or phonological therapy, is designed to accelerate the child's phonological development. What phonological therapy aims to do is to systematically help the child in learning the sounds of the language and how they are organised for speech. It is designed to help the child become an active problem solver in untangling their disordered speech patterns and replacing them with correctly organised ones, and it guides parents as helpers in this process. The ultimate aim in therapy is for the child to catch up phonologically, and achieve clear, intelligible speech, typical of a child of the same age with normal speech development.

Family education is the first and key component of the therapy regime, and starts with an understanding of the normal stages of speech and language development. Tables 1 and 2 include a summary of aspects of language development. Some of the terminology and jargon, and possibly the presence of phonetic symbols, may be daunting and confusing at first, but they are included in the interests of accuracy.

Table 1 Expressive language development

Age	Language progress
By 6 months	variety of cries, sounds and intonations
By 12 months	babbles CONSONANT + VOWEL (e.g. 'babababa')
	says 1 or 2 words
	combines sounds with gestures (e.g. points and says 'uhuh')
By 18 months	says 3 to 10 words or more
	uses words to communicate
By 24 months	uses 50 or more words
	combines two words (e.g. 'car go', 'more juice', 'big truck')
By 30 months	uses 'my', 'me' and 'mine'
	recites or sings bits of rhymes, songs or commercials
By 36 months	uses 1000 or more words
	asks and answers simple questions
	carries on a simple conversation

Table 2 How well words can be understood by parents

Age	Intelligible utterances
By 18 months	25%
By 24 months	50–75%
By 36 months	75–100%

Not all sounds are said correctly, but the child can nonetheless be understood. Their speech sounds child-like, not adult-like.

Phonetic development

When children learn to speak they have to learn how to make the individual speech sounds and they have to learn how the sounds must be organised in order to form words. The process of learning to make the individual vowels and consonants of a language is called phonetic development. Like other aspects of development, phonetic development or 'articulation development', as it is sometimes called, occurs in stages.

THE SEQUENCE OF PHONETIC DEVELOPMENT

The sequence of speech sound development was studied by an Australian speech-language pathologist, Meredith Kilminster, and colleagues in Queensland (Kilminster & Laird, 1978, pp. 23–30). The norms they worked out for the gradual acquisition of the consonants of English are listed in Table 3.

The first column of the table shows the approximate ages by which most children are able to produce the sound(s) in the second column with 75 per cent accuracy. The second column shows the speech sounds, written in phonetic symbols. Most of the phonetic symbols correspond with familiar alphabet letters, for example /h/ represents the 'h' sound in a word such as 'hat'. There are, however, eight symbols, /j/ /ʒ/ /ŋ/ /ʃ/ /tʃ/ /dʒ/ /ð/ and /θ/, that do not correspond with alphabet letters, so there is a key at the bottom of the table to show the speech sounds that these unusual symbols represent.

VOICED OR VOICELESS?

The third column of Table 3 describes the manner in which each speech sound is produced. Each sound is either 'voiced' or 'voiceless'. When we produce the voiced consonants such as /b/ /v/ and /dʒ/ our vocal cords vibrate; but when we make the voiceless consonants such as /p/ /f/ and /tʃ/ there is no vibration of the vocal cords. All the vowels and most of the consonants are voiced.

Table 3 Normal phonetic development

Average age by which the speech sound listed is 75% 'correct' during a child's speech	Speech sounds written in phonetic symbols	Manner in which speech sounds are produced
3 years	h	voiceless fricative
	ʒ	voiced fricative
	j w	voiced glides
	ŋ m n	voiced nasals
	p k t	voiceless stops
	b g d	voiced stops
3 years 6 months	f	voiceless fricative
4 years	l	voiced liquid
	ʃ	voiceless fricative
	tʃ	voiceless affricate
4 years 6 months	dʒ	voiced affricate
	s	voiceless fricative
	z	voiced fricative
5 years	r	voiced liquid
6 years	v	voiced fricative
8 years	ð	voiced fricative
8 years 6 months	θ	voiceless fricative

Key to phonetic symbols The following phonetic symbols represent the sounds that are underlined in the words next to them. For example, /j/ represents the 'y' sound in the word 'you'. All the vowels and consonants of a language can be written in phonetic symbols.

j = you   ʒ = measure   ŋ = sing   ʃ = she
tʃ = chair   dʒ = jump   ð = this   θ = think

PATTERNS OF SPEECH SOUNDS

Linguists and speech-language pathologists are fond of saying that speech sounds in languages form patterns. One of the most readily recognised sets of patterns relates to the many voiced and voiceless pairs of sounds that occur in English.

All the voiceless consonants have a voiced partner, or 'cognate' as it is called. The two sounds in the partnership are made in exactly the same manner, plus or minus voice. If you say them in pairs as phonics ('puh, buh; tuh, duh; kuh, guh; fff, vvv; sss, zzz', etc.) you can hear the sound patterns they form. The voiced and voiceless cognates are listed in Table 4 with examples of word contrasts. The contrast between /ʃ/ and /ʒ/, which does not occur very frequently in English, is not included in the list. An example of the /ʃ/ and /ʒ/ contrast, in words that English has adopted from French, is ru<u>ch</u>e and rou<u>g</u>e.

Table 4 Contrasting speech sounds at the beginning of words

Cognates			Contrasts
/p/	and	/b/	<u>p</u>ony and <u>b</u>ony
/t/	and	/d/	<u>t</u>uck and <u>d</u>uck
/k/	and	/g/	<u>c</u>oast and <u>g</u>host
/f/	and	/v/	<u>f</u>aster and <u>v</u>aster
/s/	and	/z/	<u>s</u>ip and <u>z</u>ip
/tʃ/	and	/dʒ/	<u>ch</u>in and <u>g</u>in
/θ/	and	/ð/	<u>th</u>igh and <u>th</u>y

In the previous examples, the contrasting speech sounds were at the beginnings of the words. They can, however, occur within words, and at the ends of words, too. See Table 5 for examples.

Table 5 Contrasting speech sounds within and at the end of words

Cognates			Contrasts	
			Within words	At the ends of words
/p/	and	/b/	sim<u>p</u>le and cym<u>b</u>al	ro<u>p</u>e and ro<u>b</u>e
/t/	and	/d/	wri<u>t</u>er and ri<u>d</u>er	pa<u>t</u> and pa<u>d</u>
/k/	and	/g/	lo<u>ck</u>ing and lo<u>gg</u>ing	tu<u>ck</u> and tu<u>g</u>
/f/	and	/v/	sta<u>ff</u>ing and star<u>v</u>ing	sa<u>f</u>e and sa<u>v</u>e
/s/	and	/z/	cour<u>s</u>es and cau<u>s</u>es	pea<u>c</u>e and pea<u>s</u>

Phonological development

Phonological development is the development of a person's ability to perceive (recognise) and produce (pronounce) his or her language using a system of contrasting sound patterns.

SPEECH PERCEPTION

Children can perceive speech sound contrasts from quite an early age. In fact, they can do so well before they are able to say very many words correctly themselves. For example, a father playing with a 10-month-old baby might say 'Where's your tummy?' and the baby would respond by patting his or her middle. Then the father might say 'Where's your mummy?' and the child would turn and look at its mother. In this simple example we find that the baby is able to recognise the distinction between the words 'tummy' and 'mummy' because he or she recognises the contrast between the 't' sound at the beginning of 'tummy' and the 'm' sound at the beginning of 'mummy'. From our knowledge of English we might then deduce that the same baby would also be able to recognise the contrast between words such as 'tail' and 'mail', or 'top' and 'mop'.

Other contrasts might include the voiced-voiceless distinction, so that the baby learns to perceive the difference between sounds such as /k/ and /g/, enabling him or her to distinguish between word pairs like 'curl' and 'girl'. Babies also learn to notice the presence or absence of a consonant, and can make distinctions between words like 'cup' and 'up', or 'high' and 'hide'. Similarly, they can distinguish between vowels, and can tell the difference between words such as 'cat', 'cut', 'cot', 'Kate' and 'kite'.

SPEECH PRODUCTION

It is clear that small children have an amazing amount of information about sound contrasts stored in their minds by the time they attempt to speak. It is common knowledge that when children do start to speak their speech patterns sound child-like, and not the same as adult speech. However, linguists have determined that children's pronunciation errors are not simply random mistakes that occur when children try to talk like grown ups. In fact, far from being random errors, regular and predictable non-adult speech patterns are found in the speech of normally developing young children, and older children with developmental phonological disorders.

Linguists call the predictable non-adult speech patterns phonological processes or phonological deviations. The term 'deviation' is used because the child's pronunciation deviates from adult pronunciation.

Most of the deviations from adult speech patterns involve consonants, although there are many children with phonological disability who mix up their vowel sounds too. Such children might say 'bought' in place of 'Bert', or 'hut' in place of 'hat'. Children who make vowel replacements often sound as though they are speaking English with a foreign accent.

The discovery, by linguists, of phonological processes made quite a remarkable change to the way speech-language pathologists assessed phonological disability. Children were no longer viewed as making 'mistakes' with individual sounds. Rather, they were seen as making predictable child-like simplifications within their sound systems. Some of the common phonological processes or phonological deviations (involving consonants) are displayed in Table 6.

Table 6 Examples of phonological processes in normal speech development

Phonological process (Phonological deviation)	Example	Description
Context sensitive voicing	'pig' is pronounced as 'big' 'car' is pronounced as 'gar'	A voiceless sound is replaced by a voiced sound. In the examples given, /p/ is replaced by /b/, and /k/ is replaced by /g/. Other examples might include /t/ being replaced by /d/, or /f/ being replaced by /v/.
Word-final devoicing	'red' is pronounced as 'ret' 'bag' is pronounced as 'bak'	A final voiced consonant in a word is replaced by a voiceless consonant. Here, /d/ has been replaced by /t/ and /g/ has been replaced by /k/.
Final consonant deletion	'home' is pronounced as 'hoe' 'calf' is pronounced as 'car'	The final consonant in the word is omitted. In these examples, /m/ is omitted (or deleted) from 'home' and /f/ is omitted from 'calf'.

cont. next page

Table 6 cont.

Phonological process	Example	Description
Velar fronting	'kiss' is pronounced as 'tiss' 'give' is pronounced as 'div' 'wing' is pronounced as 'win'	A velar consonant, that is a sound that is normally made with the middle of the tongue in contact with the palate towards the back of the mouth, is replaced with a consonant produced at the front of the mouth. Hence /k/ is replaced by /t/, /g/ is replaced by /d/, and /ŋ/ is replaced by /n/.
Palatal fronting	'ship' is pronounced as 'sip' 'measure' is pronounced as 'mezza'	The fricative consonants /ʃ/ and /ʒ/ are replaced by fricatives that are made further forward on the palate, towards the front teeth. /ʃ/ is replaced by /s/, and /ʒ/ is replaced by /z/.
Consonant harmony	'cupboard' is pronounced as 'pubbed' 'dog' is pronounced as 'gog'	The pronunciation of the whole word is influenced by the presence of a particular sound in the word. In these examples, the /b/ in 'cupboard' causes the /k/ to be replaced by /p/, which is the voiceless cognate of /b/; and the /g/ in 'dog' causes /d/ to be replaced by /g/.
Weak syllable deletion	'telephone' is pronounced as 'teffone' 'tidying' is pronounced as 'tying'	Syllables are either stressed or unstressed. In 'telephone' and 'tidying' the second syllable is 'weak' or unstressed. In this phonological process, weak syllables are omitted when the child says the word.
Cluster reduction	'spider' is pronounced as 'pider' 'ant' is pronounced as 'at'	Consonant clusters occur when two or three consonants occur in a sequence in a word. In cluster reduction part of the cluster is omitted. In these examples /s/ has been deleted from 'spider' and /n/ from 'ant'.
Gliding of liquids	'real' is pronounced as 'weal' 'leg' is pronounced as 'yeg'	The liquid consonants /l/ and /r/ are replaced by /w/ or /j/. In these examples, the /r/ in 'real' is replaced by /w/, and the /l/ in 'leg' is replaced by /j/.
Stopping	'funny' is pronounced as 'punny' 'jump' is pronounced as 'dump'	A fricative consonant, /f/ /v/ /s/ /z/ /ʃ/ /ʒ/ /ð/ /θ/ or /h/, or an affricate consonant, /tʃ/ or /dʒ/, is replaced by a stop consonant, /p/ /b/ /t/ /d/ /k/ or /g/. In these examples, /f/ in 'funny' is replaced by /p/, and /dʒ/ in 'jump' is replaced by /d/.

ORGANISATION OF THE SPEECH SOUND SYSTEM

An American linguist working in Canada, David Ingram (1976), proposed that the organisation of the sound system involved three aspects:

1. how the sounds are stored in the mind;
2. how the sounds are articulated;
3. phonological rules or processes that 'map' between the two above.

An example may serve to clarify this somewhat abstract set of ideas. The phonological process of velar fronting involves replacing the velar consonants /k/ /g/ and /ŋ/ with /t/ /d/ and /n/ respectively. Accordingly, 'key' is pronounced as 'tea', 'gone' is pronounced as 'don', and 'thing' is pronounced as 'thin'. One theory has it that although the child makes these simplifications when they talk, they know the correct sound in their mind. Thus the phonological process of velar fronting could be demonstrated as follows, using the word 'car' as an example.

CHILD'S UNDERLYING REPRESENTATION
in the child's mind the word is correctly stored as the adult version of the word 'car'
↓
PHONOLOGICAL PROCESS
in this example, the phonological process is velar fronting, so 'car' becomes 'tar'
↓
CHILD'S PRODUCTION
although the child is thinking 'car' he or she says 'tar'

Here is an example of what happens when a child with the phonological process of velar fronting tries to communicate. Four-year-old Brian had this conversation with his father, Philip:

BRIAN: Tan I tum with you in the tar, Daddy?
PHILIP: Not tar, Brian. The word is 'car'.
BRIAN: [indignantly] I said 'tar'!
PHILIP: OK. Let's go in the tar then. [Starting to sing] Take you riding in my tar tar...
BRIAN: [laughing] That's silly, Daddy. It's not tar, it's TAR!

Often, more than one process can occur in the same word. For example, a child with the processes of stopping and velar fronting might pronounce the word 'fishing' as 'pit-in', replacing /f/ and /ʃ/ with the stop consonants /p/ and /t/ for the stopping process, and /ŋ/ with /n/ for the velar fronting process. Another example might be the word 'break' pronounced as 'bate', in which /br/ is reduced to /b/ (cluster reduction), and /k/ changes to /t/

(velar fronting). Meanwhile, a child with palatal fronting and final consonant deletion might say 'si' for 'ship'. In this example the /ʃ/ at the beginning of the word is replaced by /s/, and the final /p/ is deleted.

WHEN IS A PHONOLOGICAL PROCESS CONSIDERED TO BE NORMAL?

Just as crawling is a normal behaviour, so too are 'processes'. It is normal for a 10-month-old baby to get from place to place by crawling. However, it is considered abnormal if the child is still crawling everywhere (i.e. not walking) at the age of three. Similarly, processes occur normally at certain young ages, but their presence is considered to be abnormal if they persist as the child grows older.

To use a familiar example: a child under 3 years 3 months who leaves most of the final consonants off words (who says, for example, 'bow' instead of 'boat') is considered to be behaving normally. If this process of final consonant deletion persists past 3 years 3 months then the child's final consonant deletion may be part of a phonological disability.

Another example would be a child under 4 who evidenced the normal process of cluster reduction, saying, for instance, 'boon' instead of 'spoon', 'loud' instead of 'cloud' and 'guy' instead of 'sky'. Before 4 years of age, this speech behaviour would be developmentally appropriate. After 4 years most children will no longer have the process, and will no longer be reducing clusters. Such children still may not say all of the consonant clusters perfectly, though. Some will continue to replace the sounds /l/ and /r/ with /w/ or /j/, so that they say things like 'bwoo' instead of 'blue' and 'byack' instead of 'black'.

The chronology of processes, displayed in Table 7, is based on the research of another linguist, Pamela Grunwell (1981, p. 175) in the north of England, and provides further examples of some of the most familiar phonological processes that occur in normal children's speech, and the ages beyond which they are no longer considered normal.

Table 7 Chronology of phonological processes in normal speech sound development

Phonological process	Example			Gone by approximately
Context sensitive voicing and word-final de-voicing	pig	=	pick	3 years
	pig	=	big	
	car	=	gar	
Final consonant deletion	boat	=	bow	3 years 3 months
	up	=	uh	
	soon	=	soo	
Fronting	car	=	tar	3 years 6 months
	go	=	doe	
	ship	=	sip	
Consonant harmony	mine	=	mime	3 years 9 months
	kittycat	=	tittytat	
Weak syllable deletion	elephant	=	efant	4 years
	potato	=	tato	
	television	=	tevision	
	banana	=	nana	
Cluster reduction	spoon	=	poon	4 years
	train	=	chain	
	clean	=	keen	
Gliding of liquids	run	=	one	5 years
	leg	=	weg	
	leg	=	yeg	
Stopping /f/	fish	=	tish	3 years
/s/	soap	=	dope	3 years
/v/	very	=	berry	3 years 6 months
/z/	zoo	=	doo	3 years 6 months
/ʃ/	shop	=	dop	4 years 6 months
/dʒ/	jump	=	dump	4 years 6 months
/tʃ/	chair	=	tear	4 years 6 months
/θ/	thing	=	ting	5 years
/ð/	that	=	dat	5 years

All phonological processes are normally gone by 5 years of age. Individual children may show some variation from this chronology.

Speech–language pathology treatment

Treatment of developmental phonological disorders by a speech-language pathologist may take a number of forms. The type of therapy described in this book is usually termed 'phonological therapy'. Phonological therapy is based on the view that the organisation of the sound system involves the three aspects described previously:

1. how the sounds are stored in the mind;
2. how they are articulated by the child;
3. the phonological processes that correspond between the mind and the mouth.

This perspective leads to the belief that therapy approaches which attempt to deal with the problem of phonological disability at all three levels will be the most efficient and effective, provided that the child shows sufficient readiness.

READINESS

'Readiness' is a term that refers to a child's level of maturity, and how mentally prepared they are to learn something new, or to profit from some experience. So, for example, 'reading readiness' implies that a person has acquired certain skills which will make teaching them to read a successful undertaking. The term 'developmental readiness' is used by speech-language pathologists in relation to a child's gradual learning of the complex skill of talking like an adult.

As we saw in Table 3, speech sounds are learned by children in a fairly predictable order and at certain ages. Among the earliest sounds to emerge in speech are /p/ /b/ /m/ /w/ and /h/; later come sounds such as /f/ /s/ /ʃ/ and /tʃ/; and later still /l/ and /r/, with the 'th' sounds, /ð/ and /θ/, usually emerging last of all. If someone told a speech-language pathologist that they were concerned that their 3 year old was saying /f/ instead of /θ/ (e.g. 'fick' for 'thick'), they would probably be told that this was normal for a child of that age. It would be explained that a 3 year old is not usually developmentally ready to use the 'th' sound in ordinary speech or to correct the way they make the sound.

A linguistics researcher in the United Kingdom, Nigel Hewlett (1990, p. 32), summarised the four conditions that had to be present before a child could be considered ready to 'revise' or correct the way they made a speech sound. He believed that:

1. the child had to be aware that they were making the particular mistake (for example, replacing sounds made with the back of the tongue with sounds made at the front);
2. the child must want to change their current way of talking;
3. the child must have knowledge of the required 'targets', that is, the correct sounds;
4. the child's tongue, lips and so on must be dextrous enough to use the newly learned sounds quickly, and in a variety of words.

COMMUNICATION ASSESSMENT

Assessment of communication skills is the first stage in managing developmental phonological disorders. With 3 and 4 year olds it is customary for a caregiver (usually the child's mother) to observe testing. This provides support for the child and saves a great deal of explanation. Most importantly it means that the parent(s) are involved meaningfully in therapy from the outset. The tests and other assessment procedures used by the speech-language pathologist in the initial assessment are administered with the aim of determining how the child is developing generally in the areas of voice, speech, language and fluency. Once this is done, more detailed assessment and analysis of the child's particular system of speech sounds, that is, the phonological assessment, is made.

Assessment is an ongoing aspect of the management of developmental phonological disorders. The speech-language pathologist continually assesses progress throughout therapy, in order to plan the next step. Phonological assessment involves using phonetic symbols to write down the way the child pronounces all the speech sounds in English in individually spoken words and during conversation. The speech sample, or phonological sample, is then analysed.

The analysis entails establishing the stage of speech development the child has reached, the sounds present in and absent from the sample, and the regular patterns of non-adult speech sounds. The sound patterns are then examined in detail for signs of whether the child is improving, or whether the phonological patterns are stable, and the child seems stuck at a particular level.

As we have seen the non-adult sound patterns are called phonological processes. Phonological processes include the normal speech 'errors' that very young children make, such as leaving sounds out of words or simplifying them in some way. For example, a 2 year old with normal speech will say 'wa' for 'water' or 'poon' for 'spoon'; and a normal 3 year old will say 'sip' for 'ship', 'lellow' for 'yellow' or 'aminal' for 'animal'. In children with phonological disability, these normal developmental 'errors' persist for a longer period of time.

QUESTIONS FAMILIES OFTEN ASK ABOUT PHONOLOGICAL THERAPY

What does the therapy approach involve?

Every phonological therapy program is individually geared to the needs of the particular child. Each program consists of the following components, which are introduced gradually in simple language that children can understand.

1. Parent education and training, which involves parents learning a set of skills and techniques to use at home to help their child's speech.
2. Metalinguistic training (or learning to talk and think about language), which involves the child, parents and therapist talking and thinking about speech sounds and the way they are organised to convey meaning. This is done mainly through games and activities during therapy sessions, and at home.
3. Phonetic production training, which involves the therapist teaching the child how to make the sounds they have difficulty with, and parents working with the child at home with listening and talking games and activities.
4. Multiple exemplar training, which involves parent and therapist reading word lists to the child, and the child learning to sort words (pictured on playing cards) according to their sound properties.
5. Homework, which involves parents (and teachers in many instances) carrying out tasks with the child between therapy visits.

Can you tell how long therapy is likely to take?

As a general rule, children with developmental phonological disorders receiving this therapy attend in therapy blocks of 10 once-weekly 40- to 45-minute sessions. Most of the children require two or three therapy blocks, 10 weeks apart (i.e. 10 weeks on/10 weeks off/10 weeks on/10 weeks off . . .). Sometimes the blocks and breaks vary a little in length. Children who are progressing slowly or who have severe problems may require more therapy.

Why not attend continuously until the phonological problem resolves?

There are several reasons for breaking the therapy regime into blocks. First, it is believed that children learn new skills more efficiently if they are taught intensively for a period, and then given space for the new learning to consolidate, before going on to the next thing. Secondly, planned breaks allow for the natural plateaus that occur when new skills are being learned. Thirdly, the breaks make way for other types of learning to take place, in other areas of development. Fourthly, it helps prevent the child and the adults involved from losing interest by going for too long without a 'holiday'. And, finally, and perhaps most importantly, it allows space for the child to generate new phonological learning independently.

Will my child's speech eventually be normal?

Almost certainly, yes. Phonological disability is regarded as a temporary delay or deviation in an essentially normal speech processing and production mechanism. It is a problem that has been successfully treated by speech-language pathologists since the 1930s. Naturally, the treatment of children who have other language learning problems (in addition to phonological disability) is more complex, and their potential for normal speech following therapy more difficult to predict.

What would happen if we let nature take its course?

This is one of the most frequently asked questions and, the truth is, we don't really know the answer. We think that children with developmental phonological disorders would slowly develop reasonably clear speech if they didn't have therapy, but would continue to have difficulty pronouncing certain sounds, perhaps for the rest of their lives. One concern is that having to interact with others at preschool and school, and in other social settings, with difficult to understand speech carries with it various social and emotional disadvantages and frustrations. A second concern is that there is experimental evidence to show that children with severe phonological disabilities are likely to exhibit later learning disabilities, especially in the areas of reading and spelling. Both of these concerns have implications for self esteem and adjustment.

What causes developmental phonological disorders?

Once again, we don't know the precise answer to this question. Research to date suggests five possible causes, which may occur singly or in combination. You will notice that each of these five causes relates to factors within the child, not to the way they are being raised.

1. The child finds the sound patterns of language totally confusing and cannot make out sound details from the overall pattern of sounds in language.
2. The child's speech maturation (readiness) may be severely delayed.
3. The restricted speech system becomes habit, suppressing further speech maturation.
4. The child has poor perception and awareness of how their speech sounds, and the difficulty other people have understanding them when they talk.
5. The child has a specific difficulty initiating changes in their sound system, and knowing how to organise their sound system in a consistent way.

Could I be responsible for causing this speech problem?

We do not think that phonological disability is produced by factors such as the way the child is talked to, whether he or she has stories read to them or not, imitating the speech of another child, or particular parenting styles.

Could my child be talking like this because he or she is lazy or attention seeking?

Phonological disability is not a sign that the child might be lazy or attention seeking.

Will he or she get lazy if others interpret?

No. It is hard work trying to communicate when you have a phonological disability. It is helpful and supportive of siblings to interpret for adults what the child with unclear speech is saying. Although they don't realise it, every time siblings clarify a word, they are providing a correct model (see the section on modelling corrections, pages 27-8).

Should we insist on speech all the time?

No, if his or her gestures, sound effects, and other ingenious ways of getting around the problem are effective communicatively, and are not disruptive, put up with them. Every time the child succeeds in letting you know what he or she means, it is an instance of a successful communication, and that is very important.

Is there a genetic connection?

There is clinical evidence to indicate that developmental phonological disorders may 'run in families'. Children with developmental phonological disorders are quite likely to have a close relative who had a speech or language delay, a developmental communication disorder, a language-based learning disability, or stuttering. It is, however, also common to find that the phonologically disabled child has siblings with perfectly normal speech for their ages.

Should we have waited longer before having an assessment?

Probably the best time to address any problem is as soon as it starts to bother you. Speech-language pathologists are usually keen to assess children's speech and language development, and advise about the need for help, as soon as their parents voice concern (case-load pressures permitting). By 3 years of age, a child's speech should be 75 to 100 per cent intelligible to parents. Parents are consistently accurate in identifying developmental difference in their own children. As parents, trust your own judgment, and don't be guided by the advice of a professional who is not qualified to give an expert opinion! Remember that speech-language pathologists are the only professionals uniquely qualified to assess speech and language.

Should we be setting a better (speech) example?

Providing a good model for speech development is helpful to the child's progress. It is well recognised that children learn by example. If you talk rapidly and allow little opportunity for interruption, or for the child to take a turn in the conversation, it is quite likely that they will speak fast as well. Although it can be a bit wearing for the listener, speaking fast is not a problem in itself. However, a child with a phonological disability who also talks too quickly will be more difficult to understand, and probably more difficult to correct. They will certainly have more problems noticing their own speech errors. In effect, rapid speech complicates the situation. Slowing down your own speech, if it is too fast, helps the child to hear in better detail how the sounds in language are organised, and where the boundaries between words occur.

Can correcting speech errors have a negative effect too?

This is an important point that is sometimes overlooked. It is certainly the case that too much of the wrong sort of correction can have a negative effect, especially if it is insensitive and ill-timed. But consider this, most children with phonological disability *must* have something done about their speech in order to get them communicating effectively without struggling, and to reduce their communicative frustration. The potential for hang-ups about failure to communicate seems rather more of a problem than not liking to be corrected.

Having our speech errors corrected by a caregiver while we are children provides the basis for learning to self-correct, just as being controlled in terms of behaviour generally provides the basis for learning self-control. No-one likes the idea of correcting and controlling children, unless it is done by example, with sensitivity and good humour. If the right balance can be struck between correcting errors, praising success, and letting some errors pass, the child's self-esteem will not suffer. Correcting positively, and praising, lets the child know you are listening, that you care how they are doing, and that you are there to help.

Phonological therapy

As mentioned previously, the therapy model involves five interacting components: (1) parent education and training, (2) metalinguistic training, (3) phonetic production training, (4) multiple exemplar training, and (5) homework. In the therapy sessions, and during homework too, if possible, it is desirable to try to create a 50:50 split between talking tasks on one hand, and listening and thinking tasks on the other.

PARENT EDUCATION AND TRAINING

As well as involving a general grasp of the normal process of speech development already outlined, the parent information component of the therapy approach incorporates the learning of a series of simple strategies and concepts to apply at home in ordinary conversation, and during homework sessions. These strategies and concepts are explained in the following sections.

METALINGUISTIC TRAINING: Talking about, and thinking about, talking

When a child asks, 'What does that word mean?', or says, 'I can't say that word. It's too hard', or comments, 'That's a funny name', they are using their metalinguistic skills. They are using language to talk about language. When we, as parents, say things like, 'Say that again clearly for me', or 'Do you know what that's called?', we are not only using metalanguage, but also modelling its use for the child. Usually without realising it, caregivers constantly employ metalanguage in talking with children (and other adults).

In phonological therapy, the child is helped to learn about various properties of sounds and words, and to actively explore the way language is organised. They are helped to think about sounds and words, discover rhymes, and other sound patterns, to understand the idea of a word 'making sense' or not, and to understand what is needed if speech is going to be used adequately to communicate. The child makes discoveries about language through games, activities and discussion with both therapist and parents.

PHONETIC PRODUCTION TRAINING: Learning to say sounds in words

This component of the therapy regime is more of a feature for some children than it is for others. Some children with developmental phonological disorders can already say all the speech sounds during connected speech, but in a disorganised way. They need relatively little phonetic production training, and therapy tends to focus on the reorganisation of their sound system, and getting all the sounds into the 'right spot'. Other children can make all the sounds, but not when they are conversing. They need help to learn how to incorporate sounds that they can already produce, into their ordinary speech. Still others can produce only a very limited number and range of sound types. They must be taught to make the sounds before they can begin working them into their sound system for normal speech. Phonetic production training involves learning and practising with the therapist, and a certain amount of formal home practice, supervised by a parent.

MULTIPLE EXEMPLAR TRAINING: Listening to sounds in words

Multiple exemplar training involves two techniques: auditory bombardment and minimal contrast therapy.

Auditory bombardment

Auditory bombardment provides concentrated exposure to a particular sound, sound pattern or word type. All it involves is the therapist or parent reading or saying a word list to the child. Sometimes the words are said seriously, or even whispered, while the child listens quietly. At other times it is fun to make a game out of the task, and make the words sound funny or interesting. Sometimes parents will march or dance along to the bombardment words to children's great delight. Other parents might have fun making up impromptu nonsense verse. The word lists might comprise 10 to 15 words with common phonetic features (e.g. all starting with /s/ or all ending with a particular class of consonants such as the voiceless stops /p/ /t/ and /k/). When saying bombardment words it is important to remember not to distort the speech sounds by over exaggerating them. Examples of word lists for auditory bombardment are included in Table 8. Sometimes children are shown pictures of the words as they are being said, and sometimes not.

Table 8 Auditory bombardment lists

Initial /s/	Final voiceless stops	Initial affricates	Final nasals
sea	cape	chip	sing song
soap	cup	chop	ping pong
circle	cop	chicken	pom
silly	hat	cheese	pom
sausage	hit	jump	pom
sock	hoot	Jack	sing song
sick	cot	joke	ping pong
sad	kit	juice	pom
	cat		pom
			pom

Alternatively, an auditory bombardment list might comprise 6 to 10 contrasting pairs of words such as the ones listed in Table 9. The words are said to the child rhythmically in pairs (or triplets if there are three words in a contrasting set). Again, it is possible to have fun with the tasks, while maintaining good listening conditions, by dancing or walking in time with the words in order to help children enjoy the rhymes and rhythms the words create.

Table 9 Auditory bombardment lists using word pairs and three-word contrasts

Final consonant deletion	Cluster reduction	Velar fronting	Context sensitive voicing
boat bow boat	glow low	car tar	bowl pole pole
moon moo moon	black back	cap tap	buy pie pie
couch cow couch	steam team	corn torn	big pig pig
	clip lip	kite tight	beep peep peep
	ski key	call tall	gum come come
	spit pit	key tea	zoo Sue Sue
Word-final devoicing	**Palato-alveolar fronting**	**Stopping of fricatives**	**Stopping of affricates**
weed wheat	ship sip	fat pat	chin tin
wag whack	sheet seat	feel peel	chair tear
pig pick	shoe Sue	fill pill	chip tip
cub cup	shell sell	full pull	chop top
Marge march	show sew	fall Paul	cheese tease
feed feet	short sort	foal pole	chick tick
cab cap		ship tip	
tag tack		shoe two	
buzz bus		sew toe	

Minimal contrast therapy

Minimal contrast therapy incorporates auditory bombardment using word pairs, and various other activities and games in which the child is made more aware of small differences between words. The word contrasts used for auditory bombardment, such as those listed in Table 9, can also be used for minimal contrast therapy. The words are pictured on cards, with the word written under the picture, and the child plays games and performs tasks that alert them to the sound differences between the words. Activities might include:

1. 'Point to the one I say': in which the child points to pictures of the words, spoken in random order (e.g. glow, black, low, steam, back, team), or rhyming order (e.g. low, glow, back, black, team, steam), by the therapist or parent.
2. 'Put the rhyming words with these words': in which the therapist or parent sets out three to nine cards (e.g. pat, peel, pill, pull) and the child places rhyming cards beside them (fat, feel, fill, full).
3. 'You be the teacher, and tell me if I say these words the right way or the wrong way': in which the adult says the words in rhyming or random order, and the child judges whether the words have been produced correctly or not.
4. 'Silly sentences': in which the child judges whether or not a sentence is a 'silly one' (e.g. the adult might say 'We flew to Melbourne in a pane [plane]' and the child judges the sentence a 'silly one').
5. 'Silly dinners': is a variation of 'silly sentences'. The adult says what they want for dinner, and the child judges whether it is a 'silly dinner' or not (e.g. 'For my dinner I will have 20 hot ships [chips] and two delicious shops [chops]').
6. 'Shake-ups and match-ups': a game in which the child is presented first with four picture cards such as car/calf and tie/tight. The word pairs are repeated to the child several times, and then the picture cards are put into a container and shaken up. The child is then asked to take the cards out of the container and arrange them on the table 'the same as they were before' (i.e. in pairs).

HOMEWORK

Homework usually takes the form of talking and listening games and activities. It is important that homework sessions are regular, brief, positive and enjoyable. The homework activities are outlined by the speech-language pathologist week by week in an exercise book (the 'speech book'). Each child's book is individually tailored to his or her specific needs and interests, so that no two are exactly the same. It is helpful if parents and teachers can 'sell' the speech book to the child as something very special and important. To emphasise the individuality of the speech books and to make them attractive to the children, they can include some of the child's own drawings, drawings or photographs of family members, and favourite fictional characters.

Homework sessions

Homework routines last for 5 to 7 minutes, and are done once, twice or three times daily, depending what the speech-language pathologist suggests. A typical homework session includes:

1. auditory bombardment;
2. a minimal contrast task (e.g. sorting cards into pairs);
3. a judgment of correctness task (e.g. 'You be the teacher and tell me if I say these words the right way or the wrong way');
4. listening to a tape of part of the preceding therapy consultation;
5. more auditory bombardment.

In addition to the set tasks to be done during the 5 to 7-minute homework sessions, the speech-language pathologist often gives parents and teachers a general task to be carried out as suitable opportunities arise throughout the week. For instance, parents and teachers might be asked to concentrate on modelling and reinforcing a particular behaviour (e.g. including consonants at the ends of words, or doing revisions and repairs).

The role of preschool and school teachers

Preschool and school teachers can play a vital role in the management of phonological disability. Because it is a language disorder that affects children's ability to develop easily understood speech by the time they are 4 years old, and which can also affect their ability to learn to read and spell in the normal way, it is of great concern and interest to many teachers.

Like speech-language pathologists, teachers are becoming increasingly knowledgeable about phonological development and phonological awareness, and many outmoded ideas about speech, reading and spelling are being discarded from our professional literature. We now know that phonological disability involves a difficulty in learning and organising all the sounds needed for clear speech, reading and spelling.

In the past phonological disability was termed a functional articulation disorder, and the connections between learning to speak clearly and learning basic school work, such as reading, reading comprehension, spelling and written expression, were not well recognised. However, the term functional articulation disorder is falling into disuse, as children with phonological disability are usually able to use, or be quickly taught to use, all the sounds needed for clear speech, thus demonstrating that they do not have a problem with articulation as such.

PRESCHOOL

The management of phonological disability can be greatly helped by the child attending preschool, and by specific tasks and activities, outlined by the speech-language pathologist, and carried out at preschool by the teacher, special needs teacher, or resource helper. There are enormous individual differences between children with phonological disability, and each therapy program is tailor-made. Teaching the phonologically disabled child to be aware of and enjoy sounds, words, rhymes and sound patterns, through stories, rhymes, dances, games and other familiar preschool activities, is of great benefit in supporting the therapy program.

Where possible, it is desirable for the speech homework book to go to preschool regularly, so that the teacher is kept informed, and can follow up on ideas that fit comfortably with the general program at the preschool. Teachers can also help by providing accurate feedback to the child to let them know whether they have communicated effectively or not, and by constantly providing modelling corrections.

Speech-language pathologists who work with children with phonological disability welcome discussion with preschool teachers (with parental permission), and value the follow up and reinforcement they can provide. It is particularly valuable for the child's clarity of speech to be encouraged in the 'naturalistic' preschool setting, as well as in the more 'artificial' clinical setting.

Children with phonological disability are frequently first identified by preschool teachers, who are often responsible for initiating the referral process. Other children are identified by their parents as needing help with their speech, and it is the preschool teacher they turn to for advice. Thus teachers have an important role to play in making appropriate referrals. The long-term consequences of phonological disability for learning reading and spelling are quite significant, and therefore early referral is considered very important. A small number of phonologically disabled children can be managed on a closely supervised home program, but most require between 10 and 30 hours of therapy.

Phonological disability is a very 'treatable' language disorder, usually with a successful outcome—that is, normal, intelligible speech. Modern research evidence is showing that if the speech aspects of phonological disability are treated early, between 3 and 5 years, the later reading and spelling problems may be prevented or made less severe.

Special techniques for helping

The following notes relate to therapy techniques and ways of encouraging speech development in children with developmental phonological disorders. They do not necessarily apply generally to all children learning language.

MODELLING: Setting an example

'Modelling' is a term that speech-language pathologists use to refer to the process of saying a sound, word, phrase or sentence for someone to imitate. Modelling is something that is done deliberately during therapy when the therapist says to the child 'Say this the way I do', and then gives an example of what they want the child to say. Parents do it constantly also. Modelling can be formal, when they ask their child to pay attention and then imitate, and informal, all the time they are talking to the child. In a way, parents are their children's primary speech models.

MODELLING CORRECTIONS

Modelling corrections are the preferred way of guiding correct speech while the child still has significant problems making himself or herself understood to people outside the immediate family. A modelling correction is one in which a parent, teacher or therapist hears an error, and then repeats what the child should have said, once or twice or three times after them, sometimes giving the relevant sounds or words a little extra emphasis, without expecting the child to repeat the word or sentence again. It is essential not to over-emphasise sounds or words, as it can distort them and make them more difficult to listen to and imitate. Here are two examples of modelling corrections:

CHILD: When can I ride in the bow?

ADULT: When can you ride in the boa<u>t</u>?
Boa<u>t</u>.
In a minute when it's your turn.
It's a good boa<u>t</u> isn't it? (and continue with the conversation in the normal way)

CHILD: Tan I use your tea?
ADULT: Can you use my key?
You sure can.
Don't forget it's my key though! (and go on with the conversation without asking the child to imitate the way you said the words)

If you stop the conversation and ask the child to repeat what you've said, it not only interrupts your conversation, but also interrupts the child's opportunity to listen to and gradually 'file' the correct version of the word. Also, continual requests for 'repeats' eventually frustrate both the phonologically disabled child and the adult who is attempting to guide them.

There may sometimes be a place for the 'say that again properly so that I can understand you' approach—but not during the period when the child still has a lot of sorting out to do with their sound system. In fact, most children don't require much of this style of correction, as they quickly catch on to the idea of making self-corrections, especially if they are praised for doing them (see revisions and repairs).

REVISIONS AND REPAIRS: Self-corrections or 'fixed-up ones'

As adult speakers, we continually make little mistakes when we speak. We barely notice these mistakes at a conscious level, but quickly correct ourselves and go on with what we are saying. The process of doing this is called making revisions and repairs, and it is made possible because we have the ability to monitor our speech (i.e. listen to ourselves critically). Children with developmental phonological disorders are generally not very good self-monitors or self-correctors. This is probably because they don't know where to start.

When your child is ready (remember developmental readiness) the idea of a 'fixed-up one' will be introduced by talking about (using metalinguistic skills) the process of noticing speech mistakes and saying the word again more clearly. Here is an example of the way the ideas might be introduced, using pictures to help the child follow the discussion.

boat

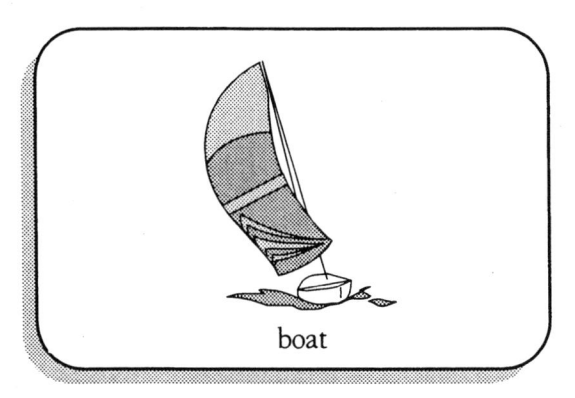

'Listen to this! If I accidentally said "bow" when I wanted to say "boa_t_" it wouldn't sound right. I would have to fix it up and say "boa_t_", wouldn't I? Did you hear that fixed-up one? First I said "bow", then I fixed it up and said "boa_t_".'

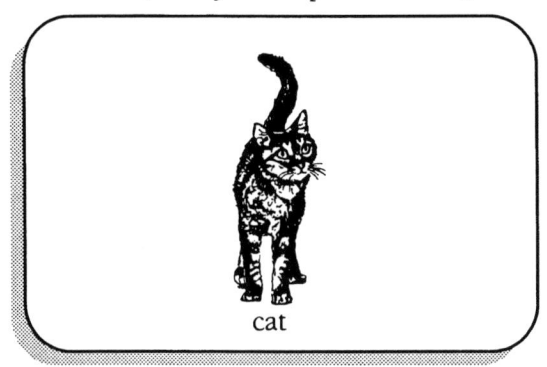

cat

'Listen, if I said "tat" it wouldn't sound right. I would have to fix it up and say "_c_at".'

butterfly

'If I said "buff-eye", instead of "butterfly", I would have to do a fixed-up one again. I would have to think to myself not "buff-eye", it's "butterfly". Did you hear that fixed-up one?'

horse

'Uh oh! I had better not say "hort"! I have to fix it up and say "hor_se_" very carefully.'

aeroplane

'What would I have to do if I accidentally said "aero-pane"? I would have to do a...' (child to answer 'fixed-up one').

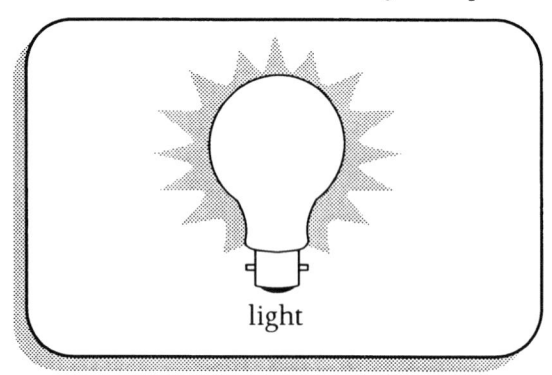

light

'Would I have to do a fixed-up one if I said "wite" for this one?'

JUDGMENT OF CORRECTNESS

Before a child can use their metalinguistic skills to perform a revision and repair, they must, of course, be able to recognise various types of speech 'errors', or the differences between their own sounds and the adult target sounds. One way of enhancing the ability to notice these speech differences, which is often poorly developed in phonologically disabled children, is by playing 'judgment-of-correctness' games. This involves the child taking the role of 'teacher' and listening for your (i.e. the adult's) errors. Here is an example of this technique applied to the process of final consonant deletion. Note that the child does not have to tell you what you should have said. All they have to do is judge whether you were right or wrong. They do not have to say the words at all.

> 'Here are some pictures of words that all have a sound at the beginning and a sound at the end. Listen: cat, cup, plane, roof. Now you be the teacher, and tell me if I say the words the right way or the wrong way: ca-, cu-, plane, roo-.'

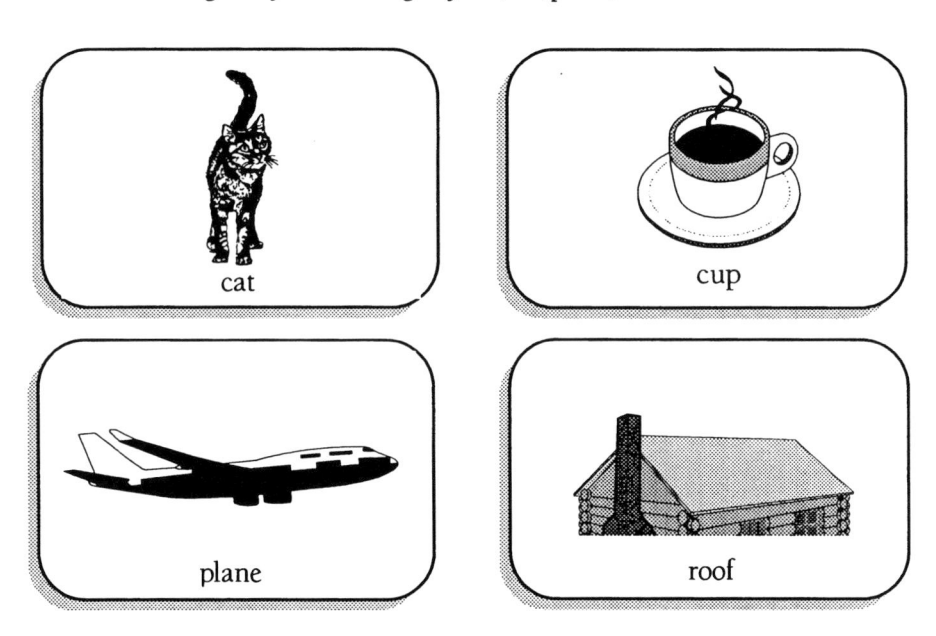

cat

cup

plane

roof

Another way of playing the judgment-of-correctness game is to play a game of 'silly sentences'. This time the child has to judge whether a sentence makes sense or not. For example, the following sentences might be used when working on the process of cluster reduction:

flags

'You be the teacher, and tell me if this is a good sentence or a silly sentence. "The racing driver saw the pwags."'

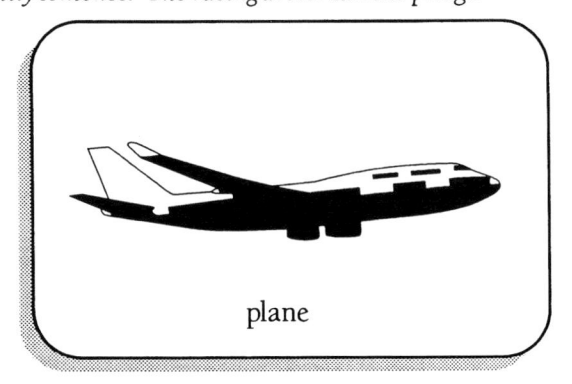

plane

'Be the teacher again, and tell me how this sounds. "The pane can fly in the sky."'

REINFORCEMENT

A learned behaviour is encouraged, strengthened or reinforced whenever a 'reward' such as praise or special acknowledgment of the behaviour occurs. For example, saying 'That's nice and tidy' when a child puts their things away is a verbal and social reward and reinforces tidy behaviour. Most parents use this technique constantly to foster desirable behaviour. Parents seem to do this very naturally, without special training over and above the training or modelling they themselves received as children.

If a child is told, 'You can watch TV when you have tidied your toys', a contingent reinforcement is being proposed. The child knows that the reward of watching TV is contingent upon tidying. In phonological therapy, reinforcement and contingent reinforcement are in continual use during formal therapy sessions, and informally at home. Some examples follow. Some of the techniques are more sophisticated than others.

Labelled praise

Specific praise, or 'labelled praise' as it is sometimes called, is a powerful means of reinforcement. The more specific the praise, the more effective it is likely to be. For instance, 'You said that nicely' would be less powerful than, for example, 'You said "car" well that time, with a good "k" at the beginning of it. I heard you say "car".' In the latter example the behaviour being admired is nominated specifically (hence *labelled* praise).

As well as being used to reinforce correct pronunciation, labelled praise can be used to encourage the process of self-correction, or making revisions and repairs. Again, it will work best if it is made specific, for example, 'That was good! First you said "Drive in the tar", and then you remembered and said "Drive in the car."'

Children's use of metalanguage can also be reinforced by commenting favourably and specifically when they talk and muse about language, for example, 'You are good at thinking up words that rhyme with each other.'

Tokens

The speech-language pathologist may introduce a system of giving the child small rewards, such as ticks on a page or 'points' for getting something right. These ticks or points or other tokens may then accrue to a level where the child receives a larger reward. For example, 20 ticks or 20 points might equal a smiley stamp or an achievement sticker.

Rewarding homework

After the novelty of having a speech book, new games to play at home, and special one-to-one homework time with a parent (or parents) wears off—and it certainly doesn't wear off in every case—the child may need a reward for doing the homework. Children will do a certain amount of work for the pleasure of it, and because they enjoy adult attention. They can, however, become bored and resentful. It is pointless trying to tell a 3 or 4 or 5 year old that the homework is for their own good! They usually seem to understand that at a simple level anyway, but that doesn't make it any easier for them to tolerate daily practice unless there is a good reward to look forward to. It is simply not fair to expect them to love doing something that focuses on what is probably their most difficult and frustrating developmental area.

Homework time can be made more enjoyable by adopting some of the following strategies:

1. finding ways of enjoying it yourself, really letting your child know that you take pleasure in the special time with them;

2. sandwiching the speech homework between two favourite story books;
3. doing the speech homework first thing, in bed with parents;
4. combining the homework with creating something with Lego™ (do some words, then do some Lego™, then more words, and so on), or combining the homework with a game (roll a dice or take a turn between bursts of practice) or puzzle (put a piece in the puzzle between each burst of practice);
5. occasionally take the homework to a favourite place (e.g. to a park) and do it there;
6. promise a special treat if the homework is done a certain number of times without grumbling (e.g. cut a picture of a hamburger, or other favourite item, into six. Give the child a section after each practice. When they have collected all six they can have the real thing!).

STORY TIME

The speech-language pathologist may lend or suggest children's books, which they have found helpful in encouraging speech and language development, to be read at home and at preschool or school. Parents and teachers, who probably spend more time in children's bookshops and libraries than the average speech-language pathologist, often discover books that foster phonological development which they can recommend to the therapist. There are many modern titles to choose from that emphasise rhyme, rhythm, sound patterns and fun with words; but the author's favourite stand-by is usually the Beginner Books series by Dr Seuss.

Some important points

Constantly model correct speech, praise self-corrections and reinforce your child's own efforts to speak more clearly by being encouraging. Ask the therapist for clarification if there is any aspect of the homework that you do not understand.

Be as positive as you can be about coming to therapy appointments and doing homework. Remember that the therapist understands that neither you nor your child would be coming unless *you* felt it was necessary. If you are feeling ambivalent about coming, or concerned about management or progress, the child will detect it. Talk about it with the therapist. Discuss any difficulties concerning the child's cooperation or reluctance to come to therapy with the therapist—but do this discreetly. Sometimes it is better to telephone than to talk about the child's unwillingness in front of them. Most children coming to therapy will go through a reluctant stage, which parents usually negotiate quite quickly. Parents, too, can go through a slump when they feel overloaded by the practical aspects of coming, on top of other responsibilities, or worried about progress.

Show your child's teacher the speech book, and encourage them to have a discussion with the therapist about follow up at preschool or school. Good liaison with teachers is invaluable. Share the responsibility for therapy and homework with your spouse, and other family members (e.g. grandparents) if that is possible. Children usually love both parents being involved with homework. It can also be a thrill (and a boost to motivation and progress) to be brought to therapy occasionally by the parent who doesn't usually come. Every now and then make the therapy day special: come by train instead of by car; have a special treat after therapy, or some other little reward.

Make it a golden rule never to pretend that you don't understand what your child is saying when you *do*; and never to pretend that you do understand when you *don't*.

Language learning is a gradual process. Expect progress to be gradual.

Research background

This small book will provide parents (and preschool and school teachers where applicable) with sufficient information to help their child's speech-language pathologist to treat the language disorder known as developmental phonological disorder, or phonological disability. The therapy model described is the first such treatment to undergo a rigorous test of its efficacy with treated and untreated groups of children (Bowen, 1996).

The speech-language pathology management of children with developmental phonological disorders has undergone remarkable changes since the mid 1970s due to the influence of linguists working in the area of clinical phonology. In many clinical settings traditional articulation therapy has been supplanted by linguistically based therapies, which take into account the systematic nature of phonology. Therapy approaches, procedures and activities increasingly aim to change phonological patterns.

The research underpinning the therapy approach was undertaken at Macquarie University in Sydney as part of the author's doctoral program. In the therapy efficacy study, 14 randomly selected preschool-aged Australian children were treated with a multifaceted phonological therapy comprising family education, metalinguistic tasks, traditional phonetic production procedures, multiple exemplar techniques (minimal contrast and auditory bombardment activities) and homework. Recognising the gradual nature of phonological development in normal development, the therapy was administered in alternating treatment blocks and breaks, each of approximately 10 weeks duration. In a longitudinal matched group design their progress was compared with that of 8 untreated control children.

Analysis of variance of the initial and probe Severity Ratings of the phonological disabilities, 3 to 11 months apart, showed highly significant selective progress in the treated children only ($F(1,20)=21.22$, $p=<.01$). Non-significant changes in receptive vocabulary ($F<1$) pointed to the specificity of the therapy. The initial severity of the children's phonological disabilities was the only significant predictor of the duration of therapy they required, with strong correlations between initial severity and number of treatments ($r(11)=.75$, $p=<.01$). A clinically applicable Severity Index with a high correlation ($r(79)=.87$, $p<.01$) with the Severity Ratings of experienced speech-language pathologists was developed, and an implementation procedure proposed.

References

Bowen, C. (1996). Evaluation of a phonological therapy with treated and untreated groups of young children. Unpublished PhD thesis. Macquarie University.

Grunwell, P. (1981). The development of phonology: A descriptive profile. *First Language*, iii, 161-91.

Hewlett, N. (1990). Issues in speech development and speech disorders: Processes of development and production. In P. Grunwell (Ed.). *Developmental speech disorders in children*. Edinburgh: Churchill Livingstone.

Ingram, D. (1976). *Phonological disability in children*. New York: Elsevier.

Kilminster, M. G. E. & Laird, E. M. (1978). Articulation development in children aged three to nine years. *Australian Journal of Human Communication Disorders*, 6, 1, 23-30.

Selected bibliography

Bernthal, J. E. & Bankson, N. W. (Eds.) (1994). *Child phonology: Characteristics, assessment, and intervention with special populations.* New York: Thieme Medical Publishers.

Bird, J., Bishop, D. V. M. & Freeman, N. H. (1995). Phonological awareness and literacy development in children with expressive phonological impairments. *Journal of Speech and Hearing Research*, 38, 446-62.

Crystal, D. (1996). Language play and linguistic intervention. *Child Language Teaching and Therapy*, 12, 328-44.

Fey, M. E. (1992). Clinical Forum: Phonological assessment and treatment. Articulation and phonology: An addendum. *Language Speech and Hearing Services in Schools*, 23, 277-82. (And other articles in the same issue.)

Fey, M. E., Catts, H. W. & Larrivee, L. S. (1995). Preparing preschoolers for the academic and social challenges of school. In M. E. Fey, J. Windsor & S. F. Warren (Eds.). *Language intervention: Preschool through the elementary years.* Baltimore: Paul Brookes Publishing Co.

Gibbon, F. & Scobbie, J. M. (1997). Covert contrasts in children with phonological disorder. *The Australian Communication Quarterly*, Autumn, 13-16.

Grundy, K. (1989). Developmental speech disorders. In K. Grundy (Ed.). *Linguistics in clinical practice.* London: Taylor & Francis. (Chapter 14)

Grunwell, P. (1995). Changing phonological patterns. *Child Language Teaching and Therapy*, 11, 61-78.

Grunwell, P. (1997). Natural phonology. In M. Ball & R. Kent (Eds.). *The new phonologies: Developments in clinical linguistics.* San Diego: Singular Publishing Group.

Ingram, D. (1989). *Phonological disability in children.* (2nd ed.). London: Cole & Whurr.

Ingram, D. (1997). Generative phonology. In M. Ball & R. Kent (Eds.). *The new phonologies: Developments in clinical linguistics.* San Diego: Singular Publishing Group.

Magnusson, E. (1991). Metalinguistic awareness in phonologically disordered children. In M. Yavas (Ed.). *Phonological disorders in children: Theory, research and practice.* London & New York: Routledge.

Stone, J. R. & Stoel-Gammon, C. (1990). One class at a time: A case study of phonological learning. *Child Language Teaching and Therapy*, 6, 173-91.

Vihman, M. M. (1996). *Phonological development: The origins of child language.* Oxford: Blackwell Publishers Ltd.